Percipience
Anthology of Poems

Karuna Sanghvi

Ukiyoto Publishing

All global publishing rights are held by

Ukiyoto Publishing

Published in 2023

Content Copyright © Karuna Sanghvi
ISBN 9789360164447

*All rights reserved.
No part of this publication may be reproduced, transmitted, or stored in a retrieval system, in any form by any means, electronic, mechanical, photocopying, recording or otherwise, without the prior permission of the publisher.*

The moral rights of the authors have been asserted.

This is a work of fiction. Names, characters, businesses, places, events, locales, and incidents are either the products of the author's imagination or used in a fictitious manner. Any resemblance to actual persons, living or dead, or actual events is purely coincidental.

This book is sold subject to the condition that it shall not by way of trade or otherwise, be lent, resold, hired out or otherwise circulated, without the publisher's prior consent, in any form of binding or cover other than that in which it is published.

In Memory of
Paulomi P Sanghvi
Dhara V Mehta

Contents

Vanity	1
Nostalgia	3
Plasma	9
Mumbai Local Grind	11
The Last Song	12
Cure	14
Rejuvenation	15
Water Lilies	19
Dance	20
Angels Take Flight	22
When The Angels Fled	24
Divine	28
Graveyard	29
Soul	31
Chemistry Squared	33
Ennui	35
Thoughts	36
A Crab's Life	37
Haikus	38
The Future	39
Exams	40

Rain in the Streets	41
Bird On A Chimney	42
Moment Of Anger	43
Hindi 44
अमन	45
गुलामी	47
शब्द निःशब्द	49
गम और खुशी	50
कश्मीर	52

About the Author   *55*

Vanity

Vanity
Thoughts take flight
Bars___long and straight
Hem us in – cage the soul
Won't let go….

A moral cage
Captives all
Veils of righteousness
Pretence of virtue
Cloak
Desires – Vanities

Fear, like a stalking leopard
Accusations – eyes popping
Knowing – the truth
Unhidden glares
And VANITY -
Craves approval

2 | Percipience Acceptance

Nostalgia

A sniff of nostalgia
In a bottle of perfume
A faded photograph
Tucked between the pages
Of an old book
Long forgotten
Resting at the
Back of the rack

A crumpled letter
Handwritten with an out of stock fountain pen
Ink still bright
Page yellowed though

A blanket with a hole
Neatly folded
Reminiscent of comfort
Security
Of grandparents

Evocative of a distant village
Where the weaver's
Long fingers expertly criss-crossed wool
On a wooden loom

Things lifeless yet
Full of lives we lived
Things that we hoard
To reminisce
For
Memories

Memories
Tremble on the surface
Of our minds
Rays of sun on the sea

Memories
Leap
Flickering flames
Of a dying candle

Memories
Echo in my heart
Tolling bells of a church
At the wake

Memories
Brush my knees
As the tall horsetail grass

Memories
Cascading in the mind
Waterfalls behind the rocks

Memories
Various hues
A sky painted with sunset

Memories
Mock
Eyes in the mirror

Memories
Shiver in anticipation
Leaves before the storm

Memories
Stalk
An eagle, a tiger
Watch, Hover, Stalk, Swoop, Pounce
A game
Mind a mere prey

Memories
War sirens
Blazing, disturbing
Warning.

Memories
Stare, Long
Through
Barred Windows, Locked doors

Memories
Unsolved Mysteries
Puzzle
Haunt

Memories
Trapped
Mind Prison
Seek to escape
With
Words, Tears
Laughter
Joys and Sorrows
Sweetness and Pain
Simmer
Masked
Always masked
With the
Present

Memories

Yours and Mine
Mine and Yours
Trapped in
The endless pit
Of
Years gone by
Years yet to come

Karuna Sanghvi

Plasma

Air vibrates
It knocks

Sound stabs
It hits

Rancid odour
Invades

Like the amoeba
It lacks form

Like the bamboo curtain
Shields
a hot post office
from
invisible dust

This plasma
It deafens
You

This plasma
It invades
You

This plasma
It is all around
You

Like dead skin
Of Ghosts
Perhaps

This plasma
Which has no form
Lives

Mumbai Local Grind

Musty smell
Pervades
As skins connect
Talcum powder, perfumes,
Sweat
Intermingle
Arouse
Waves of nausea

Languages echo
Like a dull din
All around
As
Her head swims;
The clanking wheels
Remain
The only signs
Of
Sanity.

The Last Song

His voice

The Voice

Torn apart by angst

Ripped through the soul

And left it

Trembling…. – shivering.

Desperation echoed

In

Lines_____

Wordsrunningintoeachother

Words words words-------- Stuck

Emotions e b b e   d

His voice cracked....

A living death

 Of

His self –

His

Voice

The

Voice

Cure

Rains patter softly. Long drops
Of water laced with acid

The sun peeped a bit
But forgot
Its rainbow and the
Pot of gold

His love invaded, striking suddenly
Emotions sang, danced
Surfed
On giant waves
Foaming with loathe
Storms followed
A typhoon rocked
Emotions whirled, lost
To spaces
Unknown

Words stung. All barbs
Balms
Forgot to soothe
Caress

Sweeter than cyanide
His betrayal
My toxic cure
To love forever

Rejuvenation

Reality melts
Boundaries blur
Skin – a mere
Tissue
A barrier
That we cross
Climb into
Stay under
Other's skins
We wear

We live their
Lives- those
Whose skins
We wear
Those who cover
Our ideas; our
Words but rivulets
Of thoughts

Running over
And across each other

Our words
Said by mouths
Or others
Mouthpieces mere
A garb for our thoughts
Housed in empty brains
Tingling with our ideas
Nerves spark under
The skin we climb into

We lose
We lose our selves
We are seekers
Of our souls
Bits of our spirits
Deserter of our
Bodies
Bits that live
Under the

Skin of others

The bits they wonder
In the melee of crowds
Of sticky skins
Of slimy skins
Of sticky bodies
Sinking
In the stench

Bits which linger
In blooms
In myriad pleasantries
In perfumed fragrances
Of pot-pourries
Warped into skins
We choose to live under
Wafting, drawing us in
Bits clinging
Seeking smells of other
As our souls regain

Our sanity
We come back
Back to Life
Rejuvenated
Renewed
She, of illusory plasma
Of heat
Of senseless mindless wandering
No longer wanderer
Out from other's skin
Back into the real world,

Water Lilies

Soft petals

Smooth

Floating on

Ripples - a raft.

Stones splash

Wet petals

Crumpled

Deep waters

Wide ripples

Drowning petals.

Dance

Shores of a deep blue lake

Soaking my bare feet

Calming my beating heart

Quiet waters lapped

Shores of a deep blue lake

Calming my beating heart

Cold waters lapped

Shores of a deep blue lake

Quiet, O beating heart

It's

Stillness

Stillness – I breathed

Gentle waters lapped

Mists deluged

My heart – my soul

Emotions

Cloaking

You, me

In the

Forever

Dance

Of

Time

Angels Take Flight

The minutes
Stopped
The hours faded
Time lost all meaning.

The vast space around
Stared
Blanketed
With a quilt.

A hand reached out to mine
It groped
To grip mine
In the bewildering mist.

The fog parted a bit
To let
The moon light
Upon us through the night.

The moment of truth
Stood

Naked
It mocked at our plight

That of two lost souls
Immortalised
Forever
As even their angels took flight.

When The Angels Fled

When the angels fled
A new love began
In
The dark
The deep
Devils lair

When the angels fled a
A new love began

Her hands spared
No place on me
The dark tongue licked
Flicked
Her eyes glowered screamed
And looked too benign

When the angels fled
A new love began
Her fingers grasped
Her throat in vain
Her eyes pierced
His soul
To kill
The flickering flame
In his heart

Her scream went loud
And died out in the end
After her long nails
Slit her throat veins bulged and split
Blood flowed gently at first
Spluttering and then a steady tickle

Her eyes stared up
Vacant of any life
Eyeballs bulging till they lost all colour
Her head hung horrendously on the recliner

Her body limp half falling on floor

The angels fled
As new love begun
Her soul left her body
It danced in the air
Bearing her form
The eyes stared vacantly
Out of a formless face
Long wispy fingers
Curled
Caressing my face
Touch of cold wind
Invoking an equal coldness in my heart

Nothing besides
A red vertical line
A frozen drop
Where her lips should be
A long tooth
That is who she was now

A vampire
Her fingers had a nail
It dug into my throat
Her tooth got larger and
My head fell backwards

When the angels fled
A new love begun

Divine

Into your arms. Lord Divine

Lies my final refuge

Beyond tomorrow

In thy arms, Lord Divine

Lies our final refuge

Beyond all future

Stretch they arms, Lord Divine

Call -

To our final refuge

Beyond all futures

Graveyard

Her body is a graveyard.

A collection

Of unmarked graves

Of unknown soldiers

From unknown wars.

Her body is a graveyard.

A collection

Of unknown ghosts.

All those shot

By the single bullet.

Her body is the graveyard

Where life still exists

Fresh as the flowers

Sprouting from their graves.

Her body is this graveyard

Where forever they lie buried.

Soul

Death hovered - waiting.

At last his eyes opened

And the light passed out.

The soul

Over the body -

Cold and dead.

The body

And

The soul

Percipience

The soul

And

The body

Check-mating each other

On the game-board of time.

Chemistry Squared

Pulse points vibrate
Resonate
with forgotten
Sounds of
Human Voices

Wing beats
fluttering
Just an
Overactive
Thyroid gland,
Perhaps

A grip on the
Waist. Hand.
Is it a ghost?
Pounding

Heart, loudly-fast
Sea sounds
A submarine
High BP or
My emotions

Gaseous Reactions, all.

Chemistry
Is Nothing.
Simply
Gas Talking.

Soul gets nirvana
Gas evaporates
Death.
Body in fire
Ashes to minerals
Chemistry Squared.

Ennui

Soft laziness

Conquering from within

Refusing to listen

To The resounding background

Of subdued din

The monotonous drone

Of the roll call

Shaken into a momentary attention

As my numbered self

Rang through the class

Reverberating – categorizing.

Thoughts

Tattered thoughts

Put haphazardly together

On a crumpled sheet of paper

Marred by inkblots

Squiggles. …Blanks

Where the pen refused to write

Staring up at her

Like past remnants.

A Crab's Life

Surf descends rapidly
Cloaking you, I, with darkness
Until tides ebb

Red crabby feet sift
Sand gives way to foamy, White Ocean
Time is to lay eggs

The sea, the sea, the beautiful sea
The savage, the untamed, the unbridled sea
The grey, the blue, and the pearly-white sea
In thy arms is eternal rest, O sea!

Haikus

The Future

Coal – black clouds invading
The gray pallor of the sky
Cloud burst- rainbow's gold.

Exams

Writing reams of paper
Inked with thoughts
Like a constant exodus from
The fax machine.

Rain in the Streets

Drip – drippety drip
Rain slithering off the roof
Drenching the kitten

Bird On A Chimney

The tiny wren sat
Silhouetted against the sky
A speck in the smoke

Moment Of Anger

Passion wells up
Suffocating
Heart bursts free
Of rib-cage prison

Hindi

अमन

सुबह का सूरज छाने लगा था
रात का चन्द्रमा अभी लटक रहा था
उजला हुआ सा बुझा हुआ सा
दोनों साथ साथ आसमान में छाये हुए थे

लग रहा था जैसे
दोनों में हो रही थी
ज़ोरो की लड़ाई

शायद दोनों हार गए
अचानक छा गए
आसमान में घने काले बादल

एक तूफ़ान सी आंधी आयी
पेड़ भी हिल रहे थे

हवां के झोके ते हुए
फैल गयी चारों और एक दहशत
ध्यान से देखा
तो यह क्या देखा
यही देखा की

समझौता की गाडी जल रही है
पटरीयों पर
आज अमन के घोसले में लग गयी है
एक घिनौनी आग

गुलामी

सज़ा एसी
है यह प्यार
जो गुलामी से
तडपते सन्र दिल
के साँसों की
गूंज है

उसे क्या परवाह
आज़ादी की
जिसे
ज़िंदगी करनी
है बसर
उस प्यार के
बांहों की ज़ंजीरों में

आशिक की
हिम्मत कहाँ
कि ज़ंजीरे खोल दे

वह भी तो
बेबसों सा,
उसके गुलाम की
आँखों के जाम के
नशे में मदहोश सा

शब्द निःशब्द

शब्द निःशब्द समझे भी नहीं। रूठ के भाग गए बच्चों की तरह।

बह गए वह एहसास पानी और मिट्टी की तरह।

अब वह लम्हे गुज़र गये।

जब मन से बातें होतीं थी।

जब मुलाकातें मीठी होतीं - जब चंदा भी पैगाम लाता था।

जब बाते भी ज़रूरी नहीं थी - जब वक्त यूंही खो जाता था।

वह सपने जो आपने देखे वह शायद किसी और के थे।

हमें अब सपने देखने की फुरसत भी नहीं; चाहत भी नहीं।

गम और खुशी

आज झरनों की कलकलाहट शांत हो गयी
आज हवाओं के झोंके थम गए
आज यह दिल की आहट गुम गई

आज चहचहाते पक्षी चुप हो गए
आज खिलखिलाती बच्चियां छिप गइ
आज यह दिल आपका नाम पुकारना भूल गया

आज बादल गरज कर बरसना भूल गए
आज यह दिल मुस्कुराना भूल गया

फिर भी कोई है
कोई तो है जो दिल के दरवाज़े पर खटखट करता है
कोई तो है जो सन्नाटे में मुस्कुरा रहा है

कोई तो है जो इनको देखता रहता है

किसी से नज़रे मिल जाए
किसी की खामोशी भा जाए
किसी का चहरा खिल जाए

फिर से मुसकुराहटों की बहार छाए
फिर से धुप से छाव मिले
फिर से चैन की सांस ले कोई
फिर से खुशी की लहर आए

कश्मीर

यह भी कश्मीर, वह भी कश्मीर
यह भी कश्मीर, वह भी कश्मीर
कितनी खुबसुरत वह तस्वीर थी
वह कश्मीर थी , वह कश्मीर थी
सदियों से छीपी वह वादियां थी
बादलों से घिरी बरफीली ऊँचाई थी
वह कश्मीर थी
वह गुल थी, वह गुलशन थी
वह कश्मीर थी
जहां नदी में तारे खेलते थे
झरने की कल कल से वह हँसती थी, खिलखिलाती थी
वह कश्मीर थी
वही बहती हुई नदियां, वही हंसते हुए झरने
उसकी मौत की ज़ंजीर बन गई,
उसकी लाश की कफन बन गई
यह भी कश्मीर है ,
यह अब कश्मीर है

वह गुल औ गुलशन, वह कली औ कलियां
सब बह गयी, कबऱ को भी साथ ले गयी

यह भी कश्मीर है ,
यह अब कश्मीर है
न रहे वह चीनार, न रही वह खुशबु
न रहे सेब के वह पेड़, न रहे सरसों के वह खेत
बस रहे तो रहे उजडे हुए चमन
रही तो सैकडो लाशों की बदबू
न बजेगी वहां सारंगी की घुन
न गुँजेंगे वहां सृंतृर के तार
जो रहा, वह है एक खोया हुआ सार
बह गये सब ख्वाब , रो रही है खुशियाँ
बह गया वह बचपन, बह गयी वह यादें

अब यह कश्मीर है
अब यही कश्मीर है

फिर खिलेंगे वह गुल औ गुलशन, वह कली औ कलियां

फिर खुशबु देंगे वह चिनार,

फिर खिलेंगे सेब के वह पेड़, फिर लहलहायेंगे सरसों के वह खेत

फिर बसेंगे रंगबिरंगे चमन

फिर से बजेगी वहां सारंगी की घुन

फिर से गुँजेंगे वहां सृंतृर के तार

अब होंगे नए ख्वाब   फिर से रौनक औ खुशियाँ
अब बनायेंगे नयी यादें
अब कश्मीर फिर से जागेगी, जीयेगी
अब कश्मीर में होगा पुन:विकास

About the Author

Karuna Sanghvi

Karuna Sanghvi is an elearning expert and writer. She writes short stories, poems, fiction and blogs. She has self-published two ebooks - Bitter Prestige and Cold Powder, available on Amazon.

Visit her blog at, *https://karunaportfolio.wordpress.com/*

www.ingramcontent.com/pod-product-compliance
Lightning Source LLC
LaVergne TN
LVHW041225080526
838199LV00083B/3359